Anastasis

Anastasis

Scripture quotations are from the ESV® Bible (The Holy Bible, English Standard Version®), copyright © 2001 by Crossway, a publishing ministry of Good News Publishers. Used by permission. All rights reserved.

ISBN-13: 978-1718689183
ISBN-10: 1718689187

This beautiful work of art is dedicated to my Saviour and my Grandmother in Heaven. You both are deeply cherished within the depths of my heart.

CONTENTS

The series of poems that are within the pages of this book, are words of expression rooted deep from within my heart during such pivotal moments of my life. The moments of life where I found myself in transition of being burdened and broken, to born again and whole in Christ.

The chapters take us through various seasons of my life that magnified the name of the Lord during the times where I had nothing but to cling onto His love. These were the seasons shortly after I found myself completely lacking of understanding what the meaning of life was, until I found Him.

I was lost, but now I am found. I was blind, but now I truly see. My Beloved and Redeemer has held me close and not let go.

As I am in awe of His faithfulness and splendour, I am full of joy in the fullness of His unfailing love.

This is my story, Anastasis.

BOAZ

THE SONG OF SOLOMON 8:4 ESV

*I ADJURE YOU, O DAUGHTERS OF JERUSALEM, THAT YOU
NOT STIR UP OR AWAKEN LOVE UNTIL IT PLEASES.*

My love,

As I wait for you, I am in preparation,

As you wait for me, I pray for you.

To be lifted up, guided and strengthened in the Spirit.

Do not rush, as a true story of love unfolds in its own nature of time.

When we meet and fall deeply within our hearts, this ordained love will be the beginning of firm eternity.

The crashing waves of hurt and betrayal left me lost in floods
to oceans where I lost sight of who I was.

The broken pieces of my heart were lost and adrift at sea,

I longed,

And I searched,

To find my heart again.

But in all of the wrong places, I found nothing.

And suddenly,

I hear a call from the Spirit,

Calling me to walk towards Him upon the waters.

And the closer I got to Him, the clearer I saw that my heart
was held, securely in the palm of His hands.

As I leaped towards my Redeemer, His grip held me tight.

I saw the blood that was upon Him, and it was revealed to me,
all that He went through just to take hold of my heart. That
we may embrace and cherish each other forever.

And finally,

I gained vision of who I was. My identity was in Him and He
was my Beloved.

Entwine your fingers into mine,

take hold of my hand and never let me go.

Wash me in your love,

wash me in His word.

That we may be sanctified, and the unbreakable power of our unity shall be glorified in Him.

I must

be whole,

within my Saviour.

Before I can become one flesh,

with another companion.

They say hide and seek is just a childhood memory.

Little do they know that in my life, it still remains.

The Lord hides me,

He has kept me so hidden within Him,

For a man to find me,

they would have to seek for my Heavenly Father also.

Some days I wonder,

When we meet according to His perfect timing,

Will you know that I'm the one that you've been waiting for,
and will you feel some kind of attachment to me?

As though I'm apart of you...

Because truthfully,

I am your rib.

As the potter moulds his clay,

So shall your creator, shape your character.

To transfigure you into the beauty of His will.

And as you abide in your Beloved,

The healing,

The pruning,

And the transformation of your entire being,

Would already have taken place,

In preparation for His divine timing,

For the fruitful beginning, of your God written love story.

Someday,

Somewhere,

My love we will cross paths.

Our Heavenly Father shall ordain a time that ignites the beginning of our love story.

And we will lovingly follow His lead,

Hand in hand,

Swiftly and soundly,

Into the way of eternal life.

Beloved,

I have asked our Father in Heaven for us to finally meet and be in connection with one another.

And I believe in faith that I will receive you.
As He releases you to find me, I wait patiently on Him.

Continually seeking His face, and proclaiming His true glory.

Though I seek Him, you will find me.

And through the knocking of our prayers, the door shall be opened onto us.

I pray that prior to our first encounter,

That the Lord causes your eyes to be set for me only,

As do mine.

I do not know,

How it feels to have fallen in love,

When it comes to relationships.

When I was in the world, love battered and bruised me

Love had torn and abused my heart.

What seemed like an endless cycle, came to a halt at the great surrender to my infinite Saviour.

And it was within those moments with Him, that He showed me what love is.

Through which, I have now truly understood that my Beloved is the definition of love. A blessing from Heaven.

Love is rooted in Him.

And I pray,

That maybe one day,

He will bless me with someone whose heart is hidden in His love also.

And we may fall in love in such a way that will bring our Beloved glory.

Dearest love,

May the Lord's Spirit fall greatly upon you,

Engrave His word into your mind,

Write it on the tablet of your heart.

In which through Him, you will prosper greatly for us both, our children and for our future generations to come.

As the Lord lives, you will not lack gain.

Father, may You transform my dearest love to walk in the likeness of Your ways.

May the meditations of his mind and the ways of his heart be pure and acceptable in Your sight.

May his soul be renewed, as the pouring of the freshness of your Spirit sanctifies him.

His mouth shall glorify You and drip of honeycomb.

He is

The author and finisher of our faith,

He is

The true author of our lives,

Why not trust Him to be the author of your love story?

The pages of your life,

Has already been written by the eternal hand of glory.

Refrain from altering what has already been ordained by perfect hands,

Refrain from reacting to situations that arises from emotions in the moment.

We must walk by faith and not by sight,

You must understand that His ways are not your ways,

Surrender all to Him, and allow your story of true romance to unfold in the hands of your loving Heavenly Father.

One cannot truly love,

With a hardened shell,

Concealing their true soul.

The shell which you built, around the fine walls of your heart

As a defence,

To not feel the harsh bullets of lost love and disappointments again.

As you open up your heart to your Beloved Saviour, He will put a new spirit within you and remove that heart of stone.

The bulletproof shielding of His love will cover you with His warmth and the grace of the Lord shall mend every wound.

Before I can ever love you,

Our dearest Father needs to teach me how to love again.

I do not wait on a spouse to buy me roses,

I do not wait on a man to support me financially.

Neither do I wait on a man's approval on my beauty to feel approved.

I fall in love with Christ,

Before I find confidence in love within the eyes of someone else.

FAITH

HEBREWS 11:1 ESV

NOW FAITH IS THE ASSURANCE OF THINGS HOPED
FOR, THE CONVICTION OF THINGS NOT SEEN.

To have vision without faith is to have knowledge without wisdom.

Scripture tells us to walk by faith and not by sight.

But why do we find it so difficult to keep our faith profound,

As we live in a world,

That is tragically blinded by deceit.

Though the waves of life may have thrown us off deck,

With winds of lost love, dreams and tranquillity,

Yahweh shall draw you out of the deep with His righteous hand and continually restore all that was lost.

He shall bring you safely to the shore.

And in the presence of your enemies, the spirit of favour and never ending blessings shall overflow within you.

The fool wishes and waits but the wise pray and proceed.

A man cannot withstand the hardships of life by relying on the strength of his own.

Allow God to fill you with His power,

And rest assured,

That the Lord

Is your strength and portion,

Forever.

His grace, is sufficient.

We often retain the habit of our focus being fixed on our future,

Do not rob yourself of time, in constant wishing of what's to come.

Be alertly present and accept the sovereignty of God.

That day by day, His divine plan for your life will unfold.

A river of blessings will pour upon your days.

Sometimes, to sacrifice is to gain.

My favourite childhood story consisted of 'Faith, Trust and Pixie Dust'

Years down the line,

I never knew it would come to the reality where all I stand on is faith, trust and the Spirit of God to move great mountains in my life.

In order to have the courage to take that leap of faith,

You must lose yourself first in Him.

Dive deep,

In His love,

In His goodness,

In the fullness of His grace,

And in the overflow of His Spirit, you will soar onto higher heights and leap onto higher grounds. As you trust that He will lead you to where you need to be.

The pressures that you are currently facing, is not to terminate you.

The compression that you are experiencing,

Is the process,

Of transforming into the exquisite diamond,

That you have been predestined to become.

Pour yourself into He who is the light of this world,

He who provides the sun and the moon,

Who gives light to night and day.

As you abide in Him, may His glorious face shine upon you,

And His light surround you continually, throughout all of
your days.

In the midnight waterfall of cares and confessions, I pour out my exhausted soul before Him.

My heart overflows with weariness in storms,

My soaked pillowcases fail to drain the continuous absorption of tears.

My bed is a river.

Though if I don't learn to fully trust Him,

I myself am in danger of drowning in my own emotions.

May Heaven rain upon your land in due season,

Let it saturate every place of dry ground,

And reach an overflow,

Of abundance.

Satan is only fixed on those who are a threat to him.

But behold,

No troubles that rise against Gods anointed shall cause harm or destruction.

I didn't realise,

That the highest waves in my life,

Would be the experiences,

That taught me how to cling onto You more.

PAIN

PSALM 34:18 ESV

*THE LORD IS NEAR TO THE BROKEN HEARTED AND SAVES
THE CRUSHED IN SPIRIT.*

In the winter days of my life,

My Lord was my only glimpse of summer.

Through the seasons, the Son shined His light upon me.

The grace and warmth of His love were the only things that sustained me.

When I was in the world I loved you,

Now that I am not of the world,

It pains me to love you even more.

To know who you are

And who you could be...

If only you weren't so blinded.

They say time heals

They say the wounds from the excruciating experiences will mend

But does that mean the ugly scars will fade away?

Only through the love of Jesus Christ, our scars are restored to healing.

We as God's creation are exquisitely beautiful,

As His children we are wrapped securely in His love,

Through His strength,

We are able to withstand the pain and burdens that lay heavy
on our shoulders.

Thank God that we can leave them at His feet.

I found myself,

When I,

Lost

You.

And my heart fell for God,

When I lost you too.

Enemies will try and make you as fragile as glass,

To the point where you crack easy under pressure.

But behold,

You shall not break.

Compression forms resilience,

Resilience results in power.

Scripture tells us that there is a time to weep and a time to laugh.

A time of war and a time of peace.

In life it's inevitable to go through various seasons in life, but no longer shall I weep until my spirit feels defeated.

No longer will I be at constant war with myself, with my mind.

I shall rejoice in the peace the Lord has granted me with, even though the trials of heartache.

Contentment

It was an experience I never understood,

Until I surrendered myself to You.

They say daydream is dangerous,

But how can one cope in a world of division,

Where love and success,

Is measured by numbers.

I look on to eternity, envisioning myself dancing and laughing and walking with Him.

After all, He has set eternity in our hearts.

Your pain

Is not a part of His plan for your life to destroy you.

Your pain

Is His way of allowing you to be strengthened,

Re-awakening you to rise and use all the greatness that has been placed within you.

Through His Spirit, you shall resurrect and reposition yourself into authority as His dearest child.

I usually handle my tolerance to pain quite well.

I numb myself,

I blur out my emotions,

I run away from circumstances.

But losing you was a state I couldn't easily escape from,

When I walk through fire, I feel the heat, though I am not
burned.
When I find myself in deep oceans, I fail to keep steady,
though I do not sink.
The fire does not set me ablaze and the waters cannot
overflow me.

Defeat cannot be found in His bulletproof wings.

The Lord has given and He has now taken away,

He blessed me with you, a precious soul whose worth is far beyond comprehension.

But now the time has come for you to be reunited with your King in Heaven.

Guilt rises when I seek excuses to weep in seasons of rejoicing.

I have become so entangled in pain that it feels somewhat strange to be released into a life of peace and contentment.

Now I am free.

Saviour

Release me from pain

Set me free from bondage

Heal my wounds

Relieve my heartache

Give me the strength to get through this life.

You are the rose,

The flourished work of art created by the sovereign creator,

The son shines His face upon you,

And through the warmth of His love and the pouring of His Spirit,

You shall grow exceedingly beautiful into His will.

Goodbyes always hurt

Even the peace of closure during an aftermath can be a stretch

The wounds you left on my heart from your departure has become scars that will mark my heart forever

My memories of you cannot be erased

They play persistently in my mind, just to bluff the reality you're not here anymore.

Your clothes still smell like you, your scent takes me right back to remembrance of your aura,

But since you've made your mark on my soul, you'll be a part of me forever.

Let Him kiss your tears away with His lovingkindness as He holds you in His embrace.

Nobody can hold you like your Lord.

Some days she pleads to her Beloved in Heaven, if only He could be right here with her, in the physical.

To lay her head, in His embrace.

To dance with Him,

And laugh with Him for eternity.

In seasons of solitude, He is her only source of comfort.

Pretending to be somebody you are not leads to destruction and great deception.

I've been through it all, and it all comes down to this,

God is the only one that holds and keeps you.

A FATHER'S LOVE

MATTHEW 23:9 ESV

AND CALL NO MAN YOUR FATHER ON EARTH, FOR YOU
HAVE ONE FATHER, WHO IS IN HEAVEN.

Worldly

And

Heavenly

Fatherly love

Are two completely different matters.

Just as a gardener waters the rose

As do You, water my spirit.

You nurture, provide and protect me.

You monitor my growth till I am transformed in the likeness of Your ways.

With Your mighty hands I shall become the stunning rose that You wish.

Abba

Let Your name be engraved onto my heart,

And into the depths of my spirit.

Because I am Yours forever,

As You are mine.

His love is a love that cannot be compared.

He runs through my veins, rushes throughout my lungs and beats so deep within the depths of my heart.

His Spirit fills me continually.

It amazes me,

That you have searched and known,

The darkest places within me.

Yet You continue to love me unconditionally.

You held me up when my earthly father couldn't.

Abba

I love when You hold me at night

At 3am where my pillows are soaked from my restless tears

When my thoughts run wild

When my spirit seems low

You speak truth into my being

You breathe life and comfort into my soul

I love You forever

Earthly fathers are only with us in this world for a moment,

But throughout our lives, the Spirit of the Lord never has or ever will depart from us.

Even beyond the mark of death,

He will never part His way.

To be a Christian is to have an intimate loving relationship with our saviour.

In freedom,

And in wholeness.

I cannot express much further,

It is not a religion,

It

Is

A

Relationship.

Just as a rose springs forth from a seed in the soil,

Just as a butterfly transitions from a caterpillar,

So will your Heavenly Father grow you into full completion
of the beautiful creation He has destined you to be.

I used to believe security was found in relationships,

And that my safety belonged in the hands of a man.

The harder I sought after men, the weaker and fragile I became.

My expectations of love were broken, unwise and foolish.

But my Heavenly Father took me under His wing, strengthened me and showed me what love truly is.

My safety,

My security,

My validation,

Is only found in Him.

Dearest Father, teach me to recognise my self-worth,

To be strong, and stand firm upon Your word.

To embrace,

That I, indeed am a child of the Most High.

He who keeps you is perfect in knowledge,

He who keeps you neither sleeps nor slumbers,

He who keeps you has inscribed your name into the palm of His hands,

He who keeps you has numbered the hairs on your head,

He who keeps you loves you so dearly; He laid His life down for you.

Rejected by men but chosen by the Almighty.

Nobody has witnessed the deepest, darkest parts of me like You have, Beloved.

To be loved at my darkest is to have searched right into the depths of my soul and shine your light on the rosebuds of my heart.

It is a sacred reality to accept that you are set apart from man to be in touch with God.

Understand that nothing can separate you from the love of the Father.

And nothing else in the universe can be measured beyond compare.

After living a life of solitude,

You enter into new world,

When you develop,

The deepest bond with someone.

Someone who firmly holds you,

Who loves and keeps you.

Who promises to never let you go.

The One who keeps His word.

In all these years of solitary,

I've found myself in everlasting love.

Abba,
Some of us have never had never experienced that sweet aura
of love.

The love that sets values and stories in hearts, the sweet taste
of honey that nourishes our souls.

Since the years of emptiness, your Spirit poured upon me and
filled every valley.

He is in admiration of His beloved daughters.

Those who have gems as hearts, minds like diamonds and their worth exceeding beyond rubies.

3:16

JOHN 3:16 ESV

FOR GOD SO LOVED THE WORLD THAT HE GAVE HIS ONLY SON,

THAT WHOEVER BELIEVES IN HIM SHALL NOT PERISH BUT HAVE ETERNAL LIFE.

Three nails pinned to a cross

As a crown of thorns laid heavy upon Your head

Your precious blood shed,

For the salvation of this lost world.

He who refuses to take up their cross to follow You,

Could never truly understand what it means to be Your dearly devoted disciple.

Realise the precious bloodshed of Jesus Christ is stained upon you.

You shall walk in fearlessness in all your days.

The weight of the world on His shoulders,

With the crown of shame above His head.

How greatly I love my Saviour,

For taking my place instead.

What's more significant than heavenly, holy, sacrificial love for humanity?

My life is a work of art, created by the hand of a master.

In through which I am His masterpiece.

The canvas is woven of an incorruptible foundation.

The foundation,

Which is found within the blood of Jesus Christ.

Through death, He gave us life.

Words cannot comprehend how great His love is for this world.

It takes grace to have patience with no limit and to give everlasting love,

Even when no care or precaution was given in return.

Even death could not defeat Him.

He

Is

Greater

Than our problems.

Devona Fayana

The Spirit of the living God who raised Christ from death
dwells within you my love.

As women we crave a love so deep,

We often look to the world to fulfil our needs.

Little do we realise,

We become blinded and forget that our names are engraved into the palms of the Lord.

Princess,

Refrain from waiting around for a Prince Charming to save you.

The deed has already been fulfilled.

That moment you come to the realisation that He loves you so dearly,

That you are worth dying for.

Resurrection

Power

Flows

Within you.

I have lived a life looking for approval and stability in the eyes of man.

Though once I learnt the significance of your sacrifice for me,

I find security.

Since my value is found within You.

It is not through works that we gain favour in the sight of the Lord.

But through Christ Himself.

My dear Saviour,

Thanks to you, we receive Your unconditional love.

Everlasting life and completion is ours,

We have eternal security in You.

Tell me

how far

you think one could go for loving you?

That freedom

That love

That missing piece that you're searching for

Lays on the cross.

He is more precious,

Than anything in existence.

To walk within the sovereign humility of greatness,

Only He knows.

THE PROMISE

HABAKKUK 2:3 ESV

FOR STILL THE VISION AWAITS ITS APPOINTED TIME. IT HASTENS TO THE END, IT WILL NOT LIE.

IF IT SEEMS SLOW WAIT FOR IT, IT WILL SURELY COME, IT WILL NOT DELAY.

Devona Fayana

Roses are red,

Violets are blue.

You are my sovereign God,

Who makes all things new.

Do not let the greatness of the promise deceive you of the journey.

A swift and easy ride toward the calling is never vowed.

Stand

Firm

On

His

Promises

He will never let you down.

There is a war in my mind.

Fighting against principalities for what is rightfully mine, through His promises.

Though,

I must approach this in victory and not for victory.

Because truly I tell you,

The battle is already won by my Saviour.

As my lips continually commend the exhalation of Your holy name,

A pouring overflow of milk and honey reigns upon my land.

Devona Fayana

We've all faced an unfortunate series of events ending in disappointments when it comes to promises.

We often place them on pedestals only to be let down.

A man is not created to be perfect in all his ways.

But I know one who is,

The Alpha and Omega who keeps His word.

No failure,

Is found in Him.

I cannot rely on my own strength

I cannot rely on my own instincts

I cannot rely on myself, to get to the promise, to walk firmly into my destiny.

I long for Your powerful wisdom and guidance

All Your ways are perfect and pure

Lead me into Your will.

It is not by your efforts only,

But through His Spirit,

In His timing,

And the persistence of faith,

He will fulfil all that He declared to you.

Do not be led by your emotions and what you can see

In fact be in alignment with the Spirit

And He will lead you to live by what you know

This is the truth that lies within His word

That is the promises given to you.

He is sewing feathers of steel onto our backs, and in completion we will mount up as eagles.

Be cautious to keep your eyes fixed on Him

Jesus said He is the way, the truth and the light

The promise may seem far out of touch to reach – but He is the way

The promise may seem impossible to achieve – but He is the way

The promise may seem too big for you to handle – but He is the way

There's a bright light awaiting you on the other side of the horizon.

May the windows of Heaven open up gloriously above me,

May it rain on my life in its season.

Let the blessings that You have ordained for me,

Be released freely into my life.

No amount of setback, obstacles or disappointments can stop
His plans being fulfilled.

Sometimes, the only thing getting in the way of your destiny
is you.

You have visions of the most beautiful flower garden but are too busy looking for others to create it.

Little do you know that you yourself are the gardener at heart, the seeds have already been placed inside of you.

Listen to the sweet, still voice of guidance and instruction. And your creator will bless the works of your hands.

Someone once told me,

That Satan is vicious

But not victorious.

It is true, he tirelessly tries but he will not prevail.

The closer the promise,

The fiercer the battle.

Gird your arms with strength and keep shielded with faith.

You shall overcome.

No darkness of the universe can contaminate the light that God has lit within your life.

The farther the promise seems, and the higher the mountains I face,

I have no other option,

But to completely and inevitably,

Immerse myself,

In your guidance.

I wait

I wait on the Lord

For Him to fulfil His promises to me

I wait on the Lord

For Him to renew my strength

I wait on the Lord

To make a way in the wilderness for me

I wait on the Lord

To fill every sunken, empty part of me

I wait on Him

As He is working, I am working also

I just wait

With an eager heart and weary soul

I will continually wait faithfully

To watch His words come to pass

Enlighten me on the realities of waiting on God,

When you have failed to put actions into place?

What good is it to wait,

When He has clearly placed the first steps in front of your sight?

PRESENCE

EXODUS 33:14 ESV

*MY PRESENCE WILL GO WITH YOU AND I WILL GIVE YOU
REST.*

Glorious presence

destroys the magnitudes of chaos.

I immerse myself in truth,

I feed myself with the word,

And through meditation, my lips drip with milk and honey.

He envisions gardens in our hearts with seeds in our palms and greatness in our reach.

Through gifting we plant and create what our hands find to do.

Then through watering for the replenishment of our faith, He blooms the vision into the beauty of His divine will.

I adore fresh air,

The feeling of the air charging through me ignites my soul.

Your mighty presence continually rests within the air, as I become in touch with the rush of it, You invigorate my being.

I adore that,

Because You are closer than the air I breathe.

To fear Him, is to be whole.

To fear Him, is to become fearless of all else.

Some days

I watch the clouds gracefully flow by.

And as I meditate on You, I remain still.

Only because

This magnificent sky is the only thing on earth closest to
Heaven

He commands the sun to rise and the moon and stars to take their place.

The paintings of the skies are His works and the blossoming of blooms is His doing.

The fine detail of a rose and its petals show the precision that lays within His heart.

Analyse the art of a snowflake or the uniqueness of your fingerprints and know that there are none the same.

Just as He cares for the birds of the sky and animals of the wild, the love is so real that He has invested in you too.

Blessed are the lost who pursue His heart, for they shall be found by His love.

His presence overwhelms me, fulfils me.

Just like the stars in the night sky rise to be in aura of the great moon,

As do I rise to worship and honour Him,

To experience the power of His might,

To know and to love Him.

Let there be light in my life,
Let Your light shine so bright, that you may be as the sun to
my life.

To live with your presence surrounding me, outshining the
darkness of disappointments and mistakes.

Allow me Abba to receive the fullness of purpose and true joy.

When I feel a rush of Your presence, it's as though I've been released into another world,

When I hear the sound of Your mighty voice, my spirit swells and warms up within me,

When I hold Your hand, an overflow of peace rises around me.

It is during those intimate moments with you, where I feel free.

Free.

Secure in the arms of my King.

.

Your works of art rekindles me.

It creates an overflow of peace rising up within me,

To know that there is nowhere that I am, where You are not.

Your art,

Your creation,

Your beauty nourishes my mind.

As I wake and come into connection with the morning twilight

The gradient of the great sky takes me into aura as it transitions

How glorious is Your mind

Exquisite are your designs my Heavenly Father

When I stop and look, I am forever surrounded by Your ravishing beauty.

The sound of His name shakes the earth,

Makes the seas roar,

Makes demons tremble,

And your enemies scatter.

He is your Lord, treasure Him.

I'm in love with the deep midnight sky, the sparkling
scattered stars takes my breath away.

Shining stars in the sky tend to remind me of fairy tales,
where the Princess stares into the sky wishing for a miracle.

My life may not be a fairy tale,

But my life was written by You.

–The Greatest.

His voice is like a melody to me.

Is it absurd that if you look at the stars close enough, within a twinkle of an eye you'll realise it's like an angel?

Floating gracefully within the air around the moon, as they watch over you.

The whisper of your voice causes birds to sing and flowers to bloom.

Seas of birds soar in the sky by the instruction of your hand

Schools of fishes rejoice in your presence as they dance in the ocean depths

Your people sing for the exhalation of Your name

The creation glorifies the creator, because You are worth it all.

.

GLORY

PSALM 104:31 ESV

*MAY THE GLORY OF THE LORD ENDURE FOREVER, MAY THE
LORD REJOICE IN HIS WORKS.*

Sometimes,

we're too busy admiring the creation than the creator.

His glory,

His grace,

His goodness,

Outweighs our infirmities.

Let the glory of Your Spirit ignite fire through my heart and cleanse every evil way within me.

Through which I shall usher out milk and honey for the glorification of Your name in all the days I shall live.

I shall rid every substance of my life that contaminates me from experiencing the fullness of Your glory.

Your presence

is Heaven to me, Beloved.

There is nothing in the entire existence of this universe that compares to You.

Truly I tell you,

The purification of your spirit starts with surrender to your Saviour.

Let His Spirit reign so mighty in your life

That every hardship you face falls down at His presence of authority.

He is truly a worthy artist of masterpiece.

Ever stopped to realise that you are an authentic design of His original, glorious creation?

Sweet joyful birds sing your song of glory; the morning breeze exalts your praise.

I was never a morning person until I learnt to join them,

Filling my mouth with rejoicing,

Showering Your name in worship and being in awe of Your sovereignty.

Through periods of consecration,

Embrace the glory of the Lord that rests within you.

Through the power of His Spirit,

He will teach and guide us into all truth.

Through Him, we are made new.

When I am in admiration of the clouds elegantly floating with grace across the sky,

I envision Your mighty hand transitioning them as they obey the sound of Your voice.

Father, as creator of the universe, everything shall surrender to You.

To my King in Heaven,

How holy is Your wonderful name?

How marvellous are Your hands and every work that is created by them?

I will forever exalt you.

Devona Fayana

He who is in me is the authentic artist of all creation that transcends from the beginning of time.

He is the one and only true God of the universe whose power is endless.

He is a God of love and of righteousness; I will forever live to glorify Him.

Beautiful, there is no reason for insecurity in your eyes.

Do not overlook The Almighty's stunning design.

You are His masterpiece,

Embrace it.

He paints the early morning sky of a stunning gradient.

A picturesque transition of colours that are so beautiful,

I wake to find myself breath-taken of His beauty.

How can one be so full of glory and great sovereignty?

To have perfect knowledge,

And retain understanding on all deeds under the sun.

It's not only just the things He can do for us that is great, it is who He is.
Appreciate the giver more than gift and open yourself up experience the deep love that He so longs to give you.

The kind of love you cannot attain elsewhere.

ELLEN VIOLA:

THE VIRTUOUS WOMAN

PROVERBS 31:25 ESV

STRENGTH AND DIGNITY ARE HER CLOTHING, AND SHE
LAUGHS AT THE TIME TO COME.

In the early years of my life, my Nan and I used to water her beautiful flowers in the garden. The colours and architect of flowers were always so striking to me; I always made sure to water the petals as priority to enhance their beauty.

Though actually, my Nan corrected me and told me I should always ensure to water the base of the plant instead. It is in the roots where the flowers receive their nutrients and the light of the sun which results in the release of their blooming beauty.

It is in the deepest part of us that we enhance our true beauty. We as a generation, try to water our physical beauty as much as we please, but let us not forget to nurture and take care of our innermost being. If not, we will eventually run dry like a starved rose.

You are the rose, Christ is the light and God's Word is your water. Immerse yourself in the Son as the Spirit of the Lord blooms you and teaches you all things.

John 4:14 ESV 'But whoever drinks the water that I will give him will never be thirsty again. The water that I will give him will become in him a spring of water, welling up to everlasting life'

Blessed is the woman who fears Him,

Who learns the true art of beauty through our Lord and not the world.

Her foundation is built upon strength

She leans on the Lord our God, our rock

She stands upon truth

And walks in goodness and mercy

Her hands give generously to the needy

Her tongue speaks life

Fear is not her portion

But favour and grace surrounds her

As beauty fills her soul

Her legacy will always remain.

Her forte was faith and her anthem was grace.

What is beauty?

I used to think it were the ladies on magazines

The girls with the most likes

The women who paint their face to perfection

But actually,

I never witnessed the art of true beauty until this moment

To watch a loved one deteriorate in front of your eyes is
beyond excruciating

But the rare beauty that is lit from their spirit within is so
potent,

It surpasses death.

The sting of death is painful,

But the poison shall not contaminate our memories.

A woman who is on fire for the Lord,

Has the burning power of His spirit,

Rooted within her soul.

The Lord reminds me that weeping shall be no more,

Since your spirit is joyfully in freedom,

Dancing gloriously in His presence in Heaven.

A crown of resilience reigned upon her head, as the glory of God followed her all of her days.

She obtained the most prosperous and gentle soul, with a heart purer than gold

How proud I am, to call her the Grandmother that I love.

The day of your goodbye will always scar me.

Although,

Healing power rests within the resurrection of our Saviour.

Whenever she spoke,

It consisted of wisdom and truth.
In all my life that I've known her, I have not witnessed a bad
utter proceed out of her mouth.

Throughout the pivotal seasons of life, all her heart could find
to sing was the proclamation of His love.

Her physicality is absent but her spirit remains.

Here's to the days, in the early years of my life when I would spend days and nights with you. My keeper, you taught me all you knew.

My seed planter,

Who grew food in our gardens and sowed incorruptible seeds of wisdom and grace into my heart.

All of this, in order for our good and survival.

Through all the twists and turns of life,

You were still very much a woman who knew how to laugh and embrace.

The sound of your laughter takes me back to my reality called home.

You created a woman of courage out of me.

Devona Fayana

The sweet aura of lavender,

Takes me right back to what was once your lovely presence.

Home is where my grandmother is.

You were an incorruptible rose,

Forever blooming in beauty.

Teaching us the art of growth and grace in life.

I try not to forget that you were the most beautiful gift from God that He loaned.

He missed you so much,

That you were sent to return to the heavenly home where you belong.

Until we meet again, my dearest.

ACKNOWLEDGEMENT

To the One who created the vision and hastened it in its perfect timing, Abba Father.

I come to You with a heart of gratitude, giving You all the glory for this work of art that You placed in my heart. And I thank You for all that was made possible for me.

Your faithfulness and unfailing love has sustained me during times of testing. You upheld me when nobody else could, to press on toward the destiny which you have planted before the foundations of the earth.

I would not be where I am right now without You

My heart is Yours, thank You for everything.

Made in the USA
Middletown, DE
07 July 2020